EASTER EGG COLORING

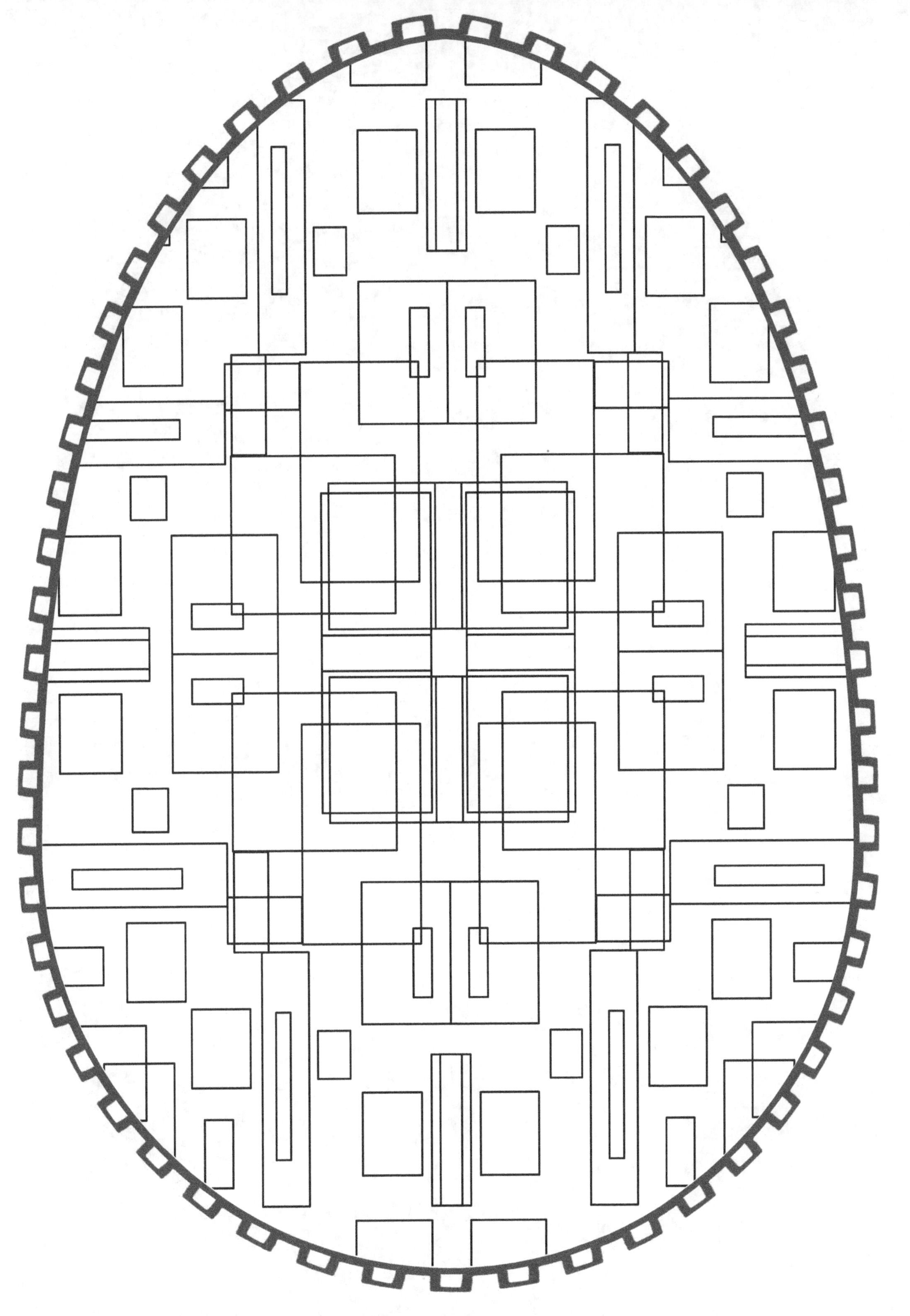

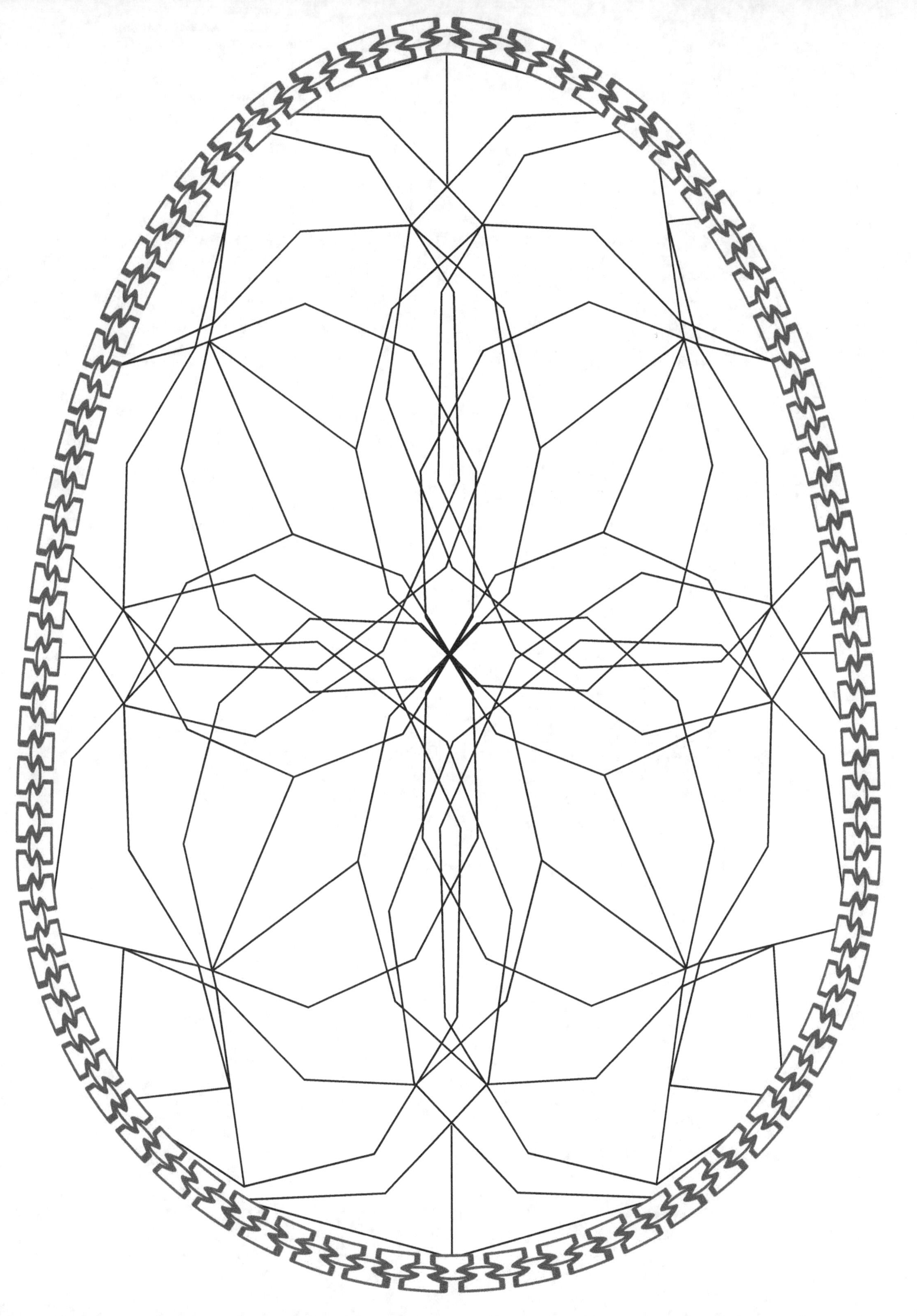

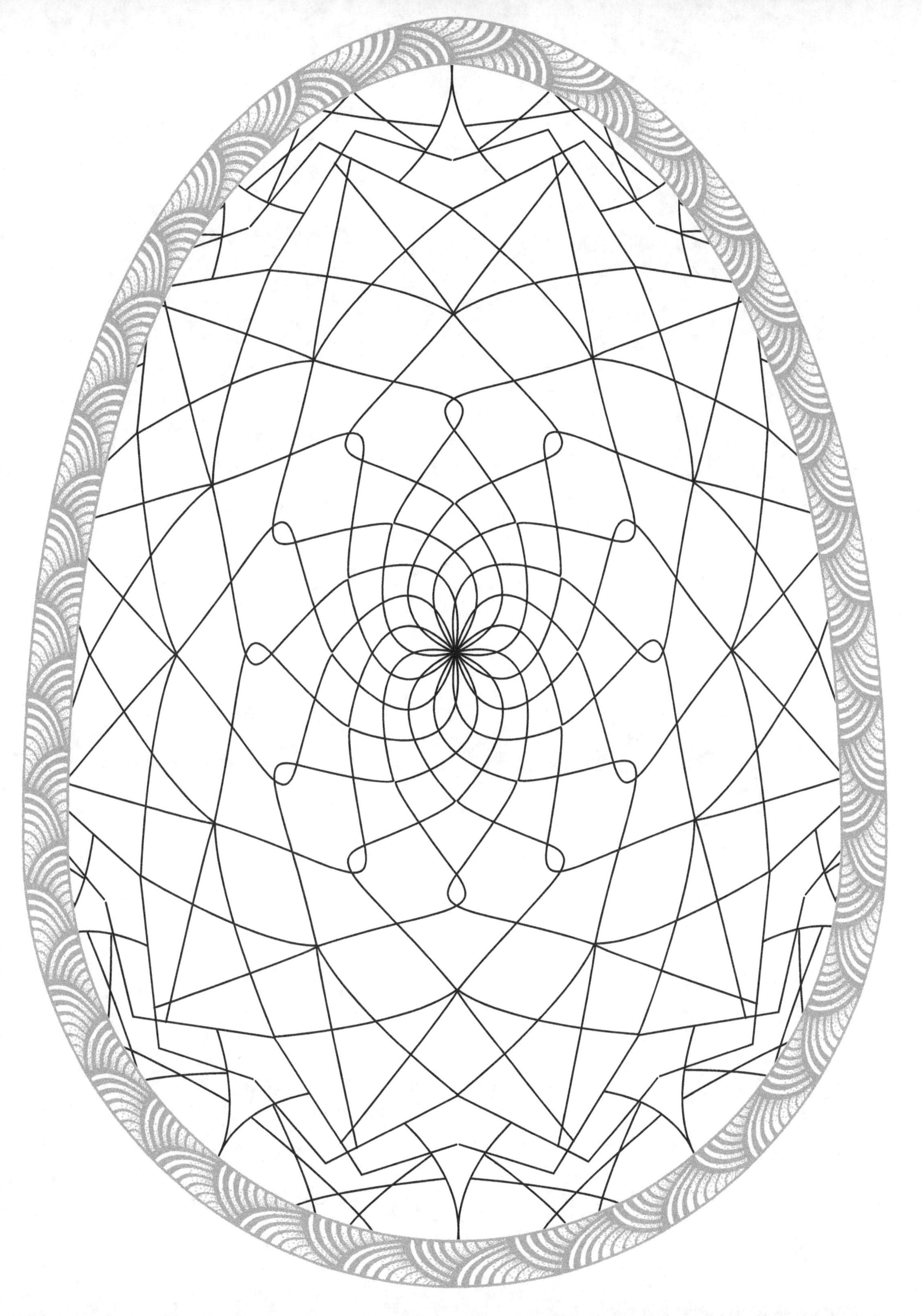

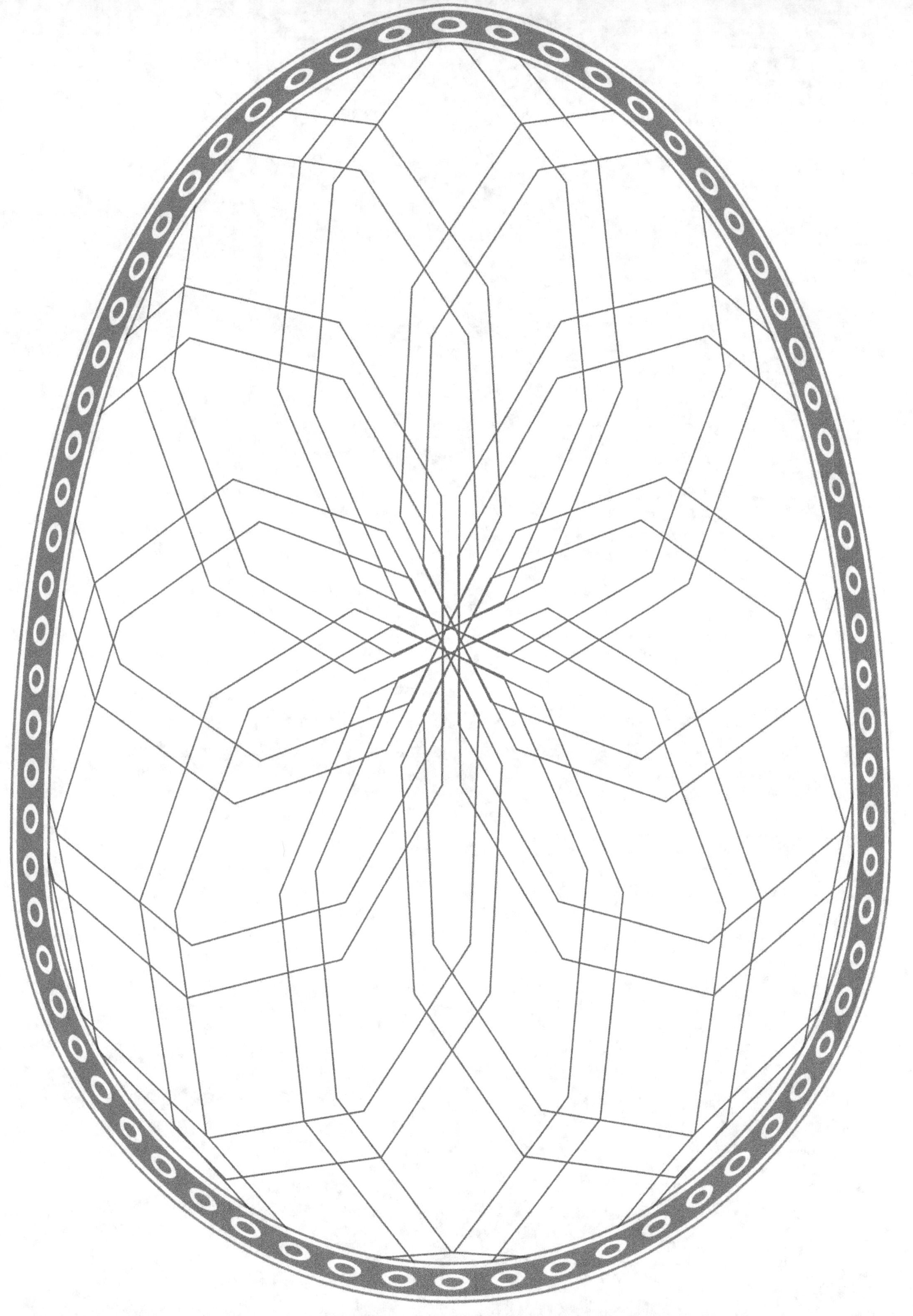

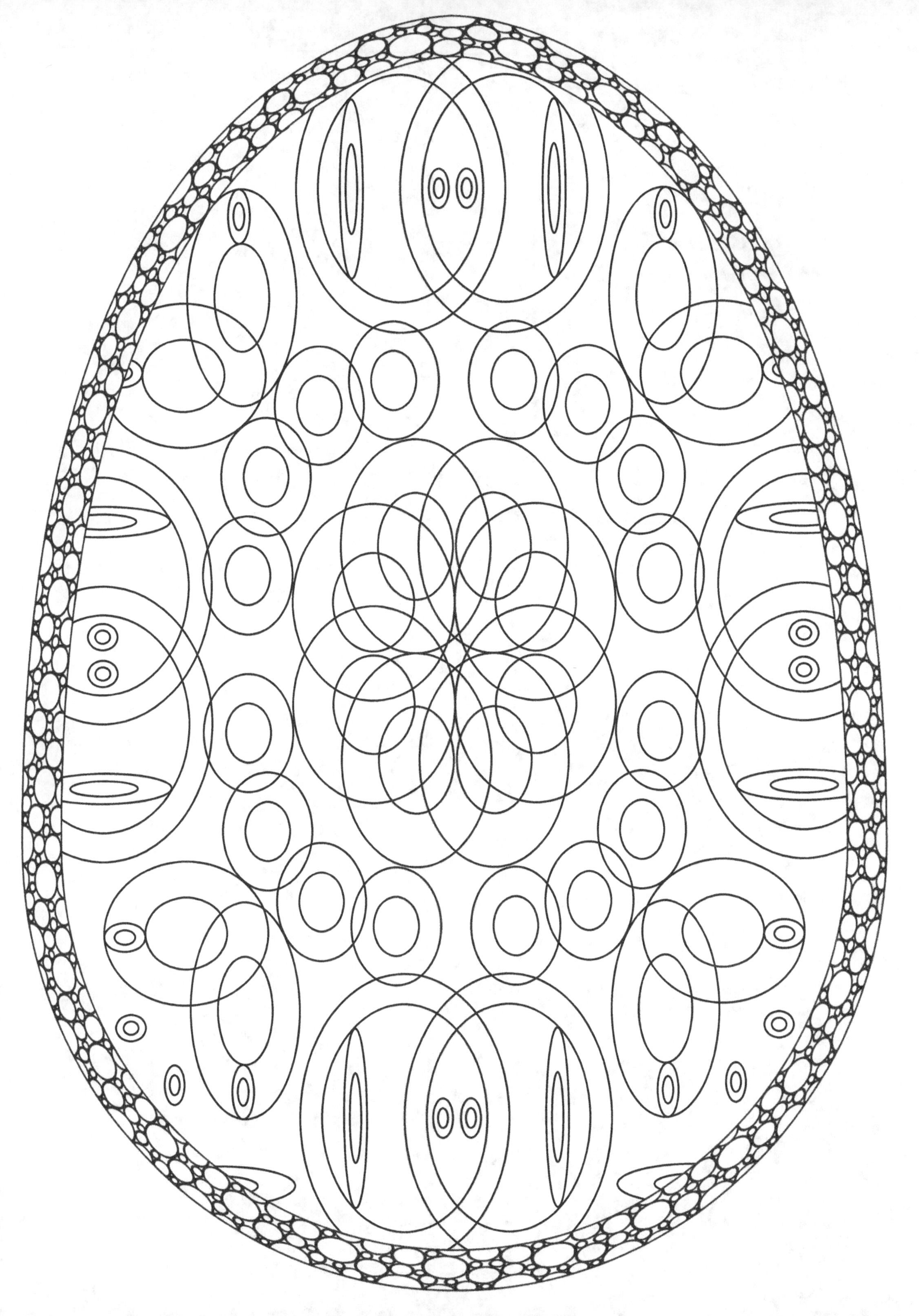

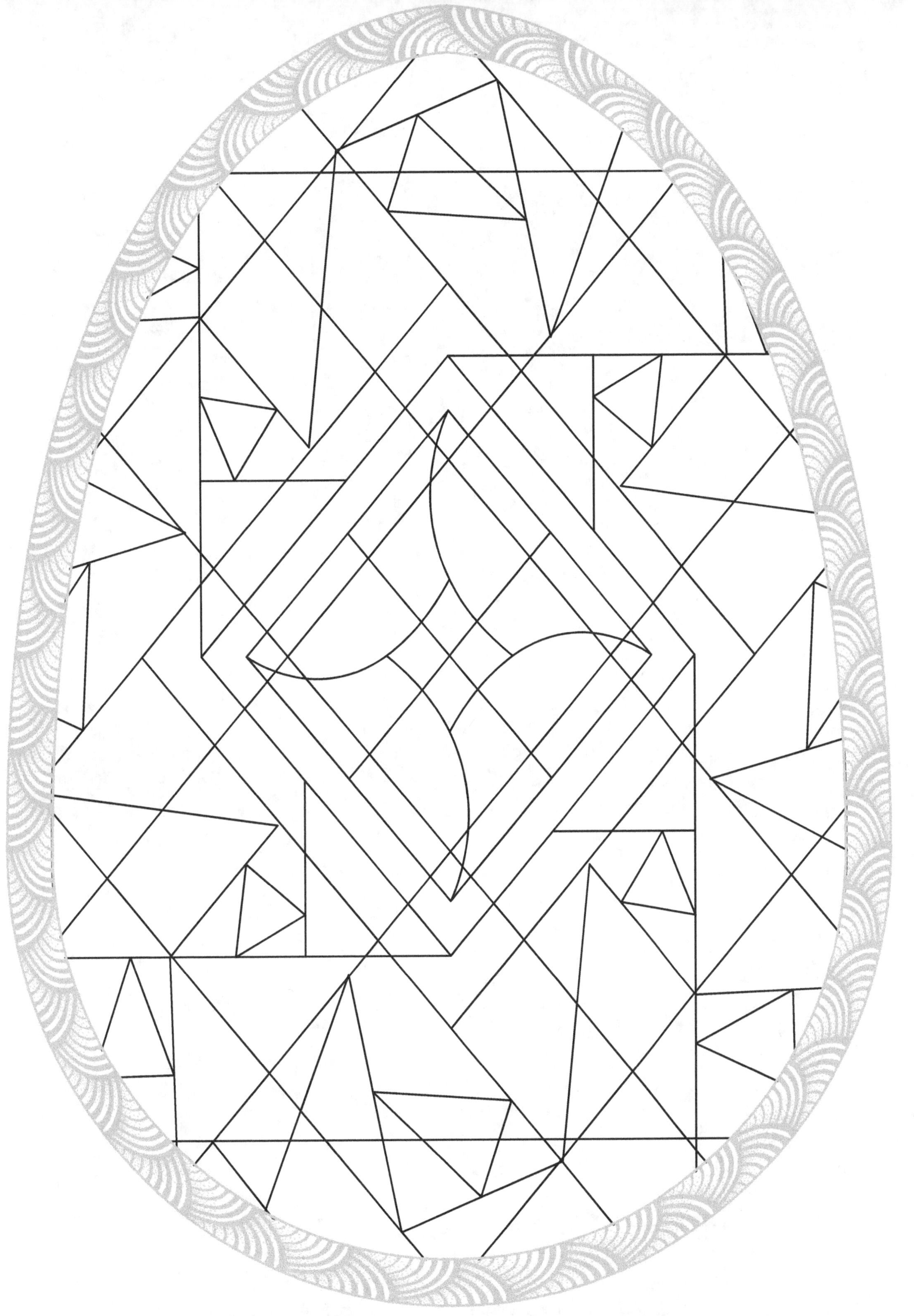

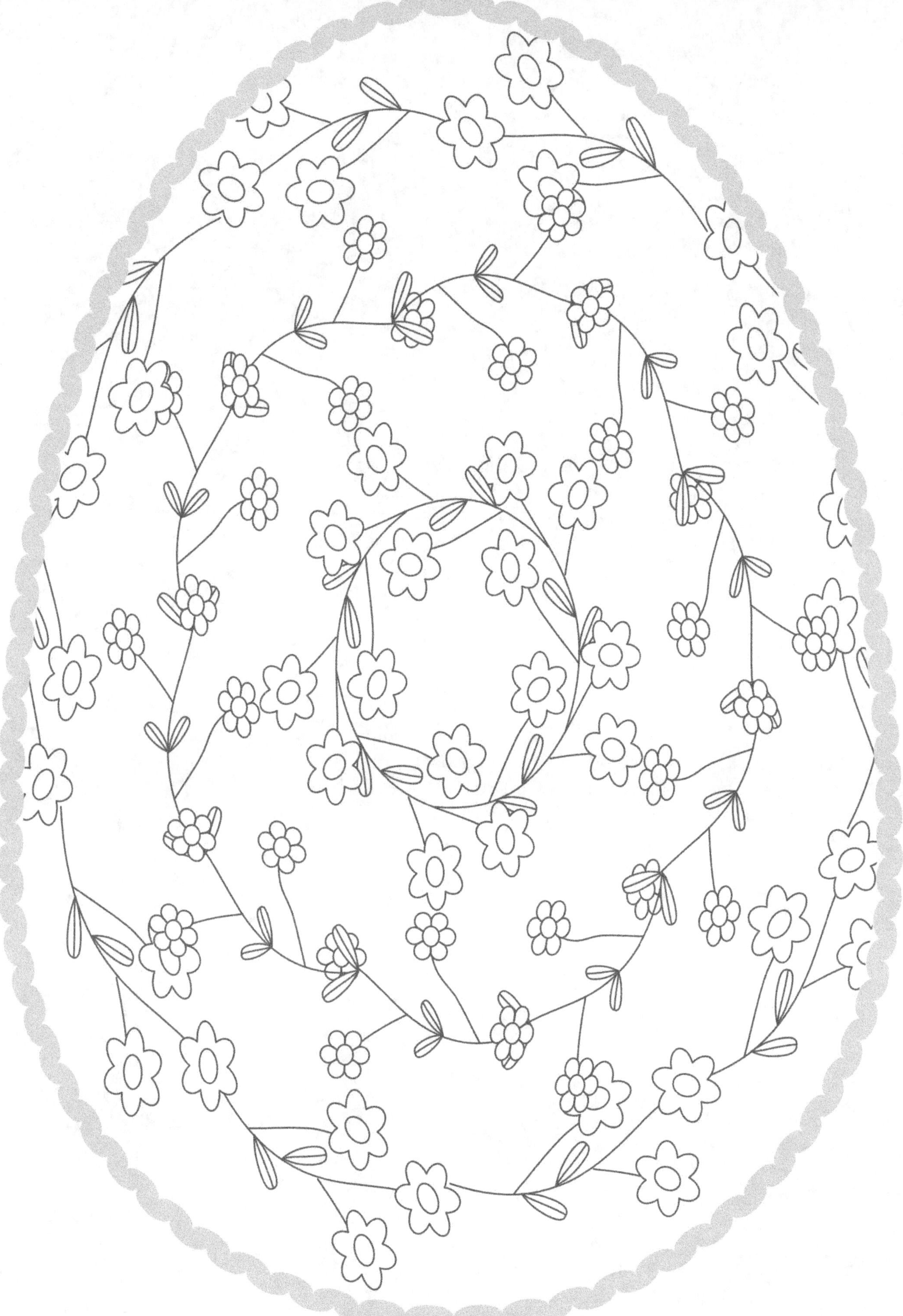

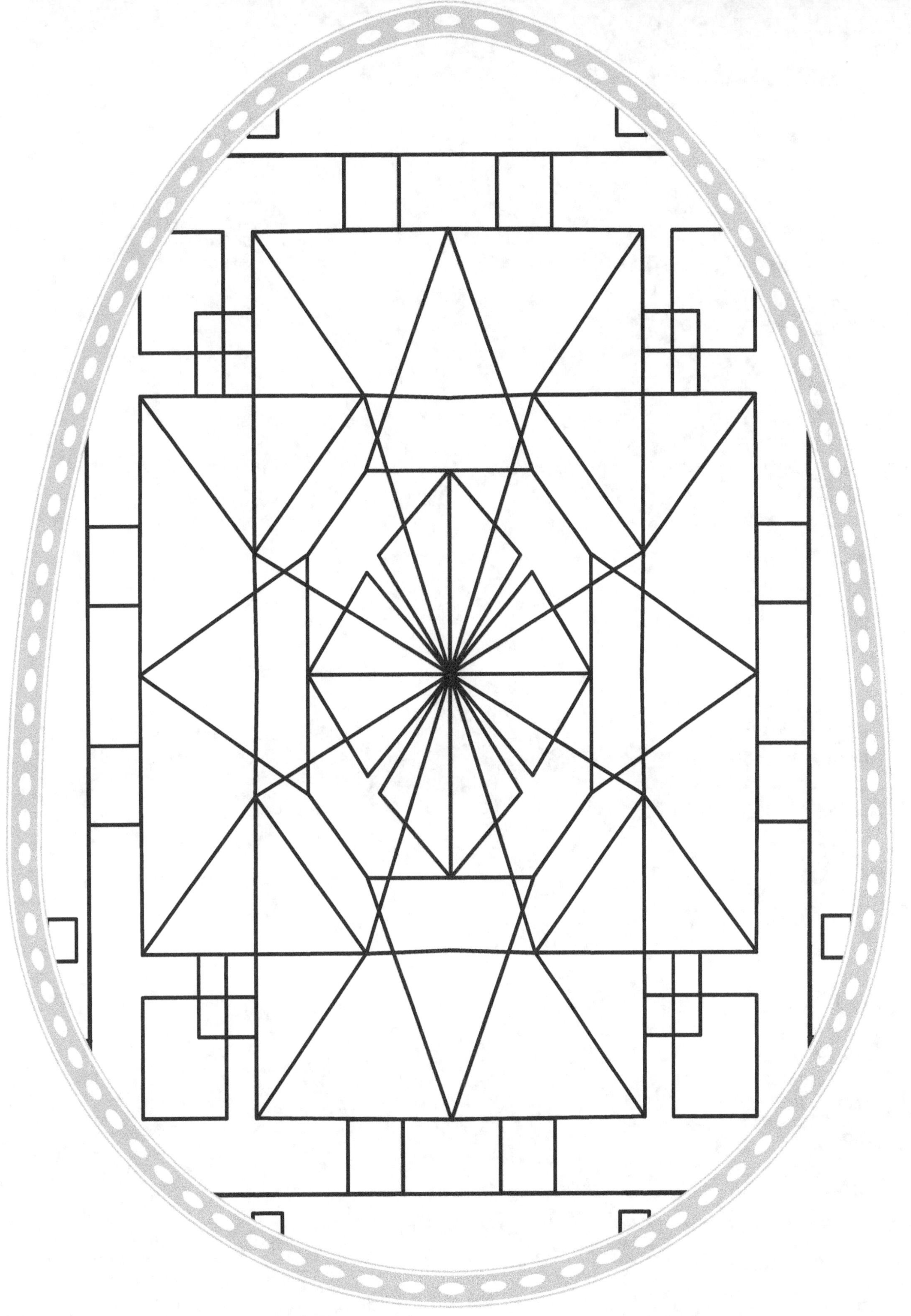

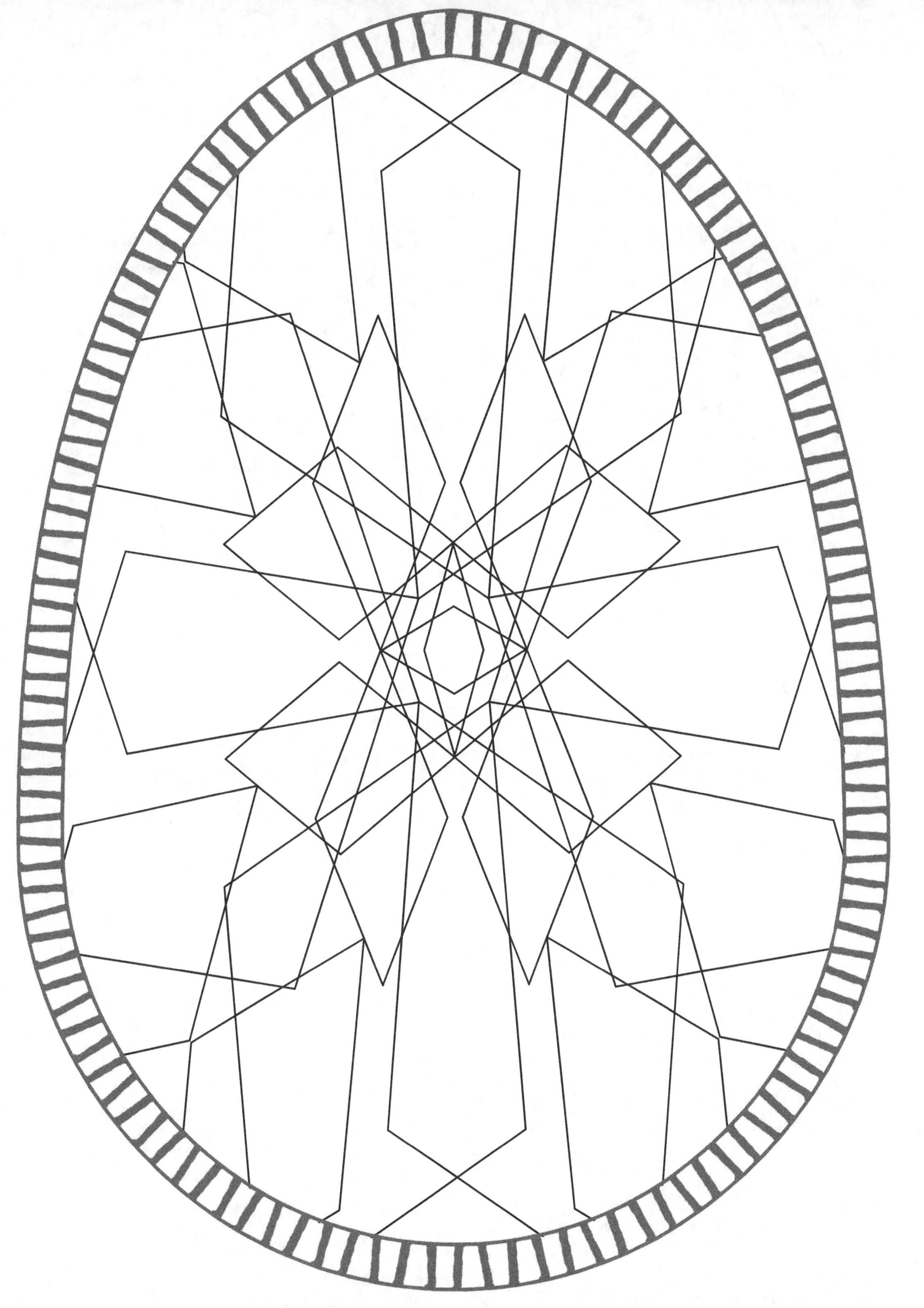

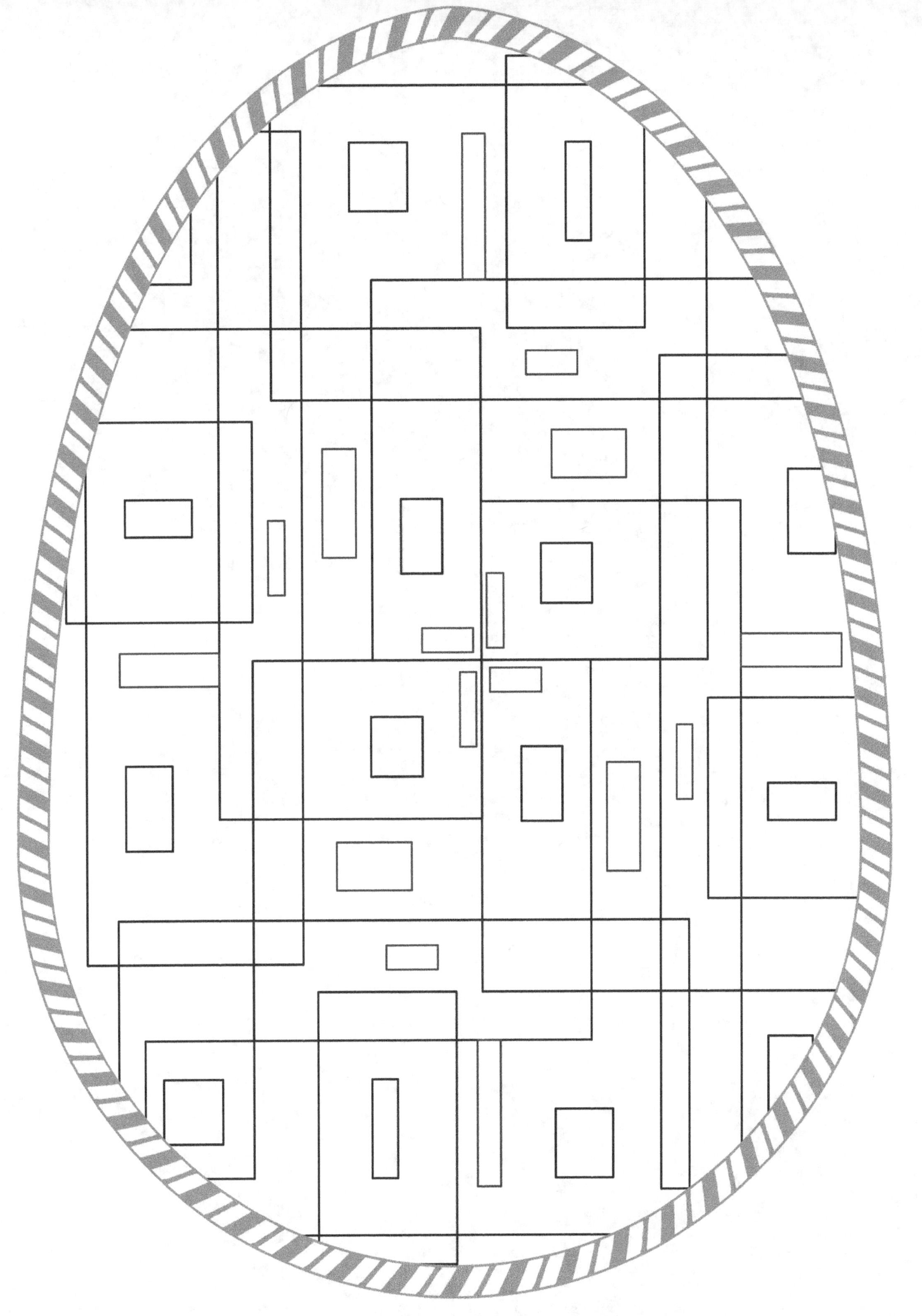